Wakefield Press

The Southern Oscillation Index

Poet, novelist and longtime arts broadcaster Cath Kenneally lives in Adelaide and spends part of each year in Tasmania.

Also by Cath Kenneally

Around Here
Jetty Road
Room Temperature
Thirty Days' Notice

THE SOUTHERN OSCILLATION INDEX

CATH KENNEALLY

Wakefield
Press

Wakefield Press
16 Rose Street
Mile End
South Australia 5031
www.wakefieldpress.com.au

First published 2020

Cover designed by Liz Nicholson, Wakefield Press
Typeset by Michael Deves, Wakefield Press

ISBN 978 1 74305 711 7

A catalogue record for this
book is available from the
National Library of Australia

Government
of South Australia

Department of the
Premier and Cabinet

CORIOLE
McLAREN VALE

Wakefield Press thanks
Coriole Vineyards for
continued support

Contents

1.

Cactus

Home by three, driven out by the stuffiness of my office
or somatizing my dread of work

dizzy, anyway, with hay fever or brain-melt

I see something is eating the new-set oranges
smart rats or possums.

Steven the gardener is moving into the granny-flat
bringing his plants along

cacti lined up against the cabin wall
rescued from the back of a lumberyard

the owner was waiting for them to die
so they could be taken to the tip

But Steven knew the cacti
have a central 'merry' channel

which stays viable when the fleshy outer
shrivels away. He's wheedled them

back to frank and open health
twisting their new limbs into odd shapes

small price to pay from their point of view
alive but twisted: who isn't?

2.

Pale Rider

Outside the cafe

un caffè bar as they style themselves

I drink coffee, observe
        trays of food being unloaded from a van
    a slew of slutty cheesecakes
                a chorus line of busty friands

in the hospital up on the hill, orderlies

stand over starveling teens
           force-feeding double rations
        doing battle with the Pale Rider

    meals are fraught at our house, too, though one night
        tension lifts as we all at the same moment
    recall the descent from the sky
        in *The Young Ones*' Four Horsemen sketch
           with a *whoomph*!
(flattening Dawn French in Mormon mode down on Earth)
of a mammoth discarded sandwich segment
                when Famine complains he's hungry
       'Sometimes God can be so unimaginative'

3.

Trench Warfare

Kenwood House:
        an autumn Wednesday,
      woods tame and endless, mild grey sky
where I wandered, hopeful, one November
        in the belted trenchcoat that felt matronly
     (from a dive in unfamiliar downtown Sydney)
      but of course wasn't on a twenty-something

First time in London

where I'd lived in my head since I could read

This time, more dogs than I recall, otherwise the same

the barrel-vaulted Stewards' Room rendering glamorous
     cheese and pickle, a pot of tea,
       my heart bursting from my chest

Still happy when we all meet at the Lion
       a drink then The IT Crowd on TV
     the others under the weather
    (under it, for good or ill, every day
        today, held under, as by a mean kid at the beach)

Another time, we stride it out to Swiss Cottage, where Swiss Tony
   doesn't live, find the gym and pool in the community centre

The day is brighter, Anna home sick. We stop at the new Camden Arts gallery
            check, then forget work email

Euroboy Gabe claims now to prefer Spain to his native land. He shows us
            his climbing wall. He'll be at our reading at Australia House,
                        common territory for now
                                        In Russell Square Garden cafe
                        select poems to read

Warm again.
            Drifting back to Karin Mamma Anderssen's lovely Camden paintings
                        spiky pines barricading or guarding a wintering house
                                    pumpkin and beetroot tones in warm, cluttered interiors
                                    We bought a gift for Tom in the bookshop:
                                                Yoshitomo Nara: 'Angry Girl: Nothing Ever
            Happens'

threatening faux-naif big faces he will like
                                                angry boy arming himself with art

Angry sister ponders the decades:
            waves of nostalgia swamping the Heath, inundating Camden
                        percolating up in noxious bubbles from my ill-sealed Underground

                                                ride it, all you can d
                                                hold on to your sou'weste
                                                belt your raincoat tigl

                                    the underrated art of straphangii

4.

Forever Yours

crossing-bells and bicycles, *Pantry on Egmont*
anything 'on' anything always a haunt of the frankly rich
none, today, encumbered by kids

a goods train passing, no little boys to eagerly watch its passage
as mine would have, as yours would have

I read lately, however, that children live on in us
us mothers, a soothing discovery

your babies' cells fuse with yours. Though

you give birth to them and they go on their way
as all the fairytales in the canon remind us
at the same time they never leave home

these are joyful tidings indeed
rest your hands over your abdomen
the babies are still there

5.

Towpath Tales

I go for a long walk
along the canal, from Wendy's
to the lower end of Upper Street

a longer walk than I calculated
this hot evening,   too far
to turn right around and return

so I veer off the main thoroughfare
find, at my elbow, a downstairs dive
Brew Box, where

the day's heat has percolated and
thickened. I choose, not coffee
but a trio of donut-shaped icecreams

one loop, green tea, one, mango
one a nameless grey-white fruit
held in shape by, I guess, edible

gel which I break into bits with a fork
and eat with apparent gusto, for
the benefit of two young

Latin lads at the counter who
watch approvingly, smiles and nods
I eat it all, nod and smile

remembering finding a tin of gum mastic
among shed contents, bought as
one lot at a deceased-estate sale

rough amber nuggets in a *Craven A* tin
unless that was frankincense
or some other outdated, pungent

stuff, way old even then,
an old man's bits and bobs
collected early last century, kept and kept

I've barely got used to being in the twenty
first, though it's getting on for fifteen years
back then a friend had a Mrs Beeton

some of whose recipes called for gum mastic
too weird for me: it's a setting agent
maybe still used, maybe in this?

Put the gel to back of mind
stride off, fearful of missing the darkening
way back to the towpath, but there it is

glowing faintly, in fading light
brisk now, heading home
regretting the ice loops

beginning to notice, as dusk falls, how few
companions I have on the path
brisker still, as fast as I can

Wendy is waiting with eggs, and roasted capsicums
the peppers' bells cradling cherry tomatoes
anchovies and garlic buds

speeding cyclists, not muggers, are the danger
they tinkle, as instructed, their bicycle bells, twice
on approach

wasted on the hearing-deficient
I look often over one shoulder
skip a little sideways hop as another zips by

proudly dodging death on the towpath
no different to doughty residents
observing grey geese in their side-channel,

gauging one waterside bar's welcome
over another, choosing none, but savouring
the choice I might make one day

recalling other walks – where was the narrowboat
that sold books? with the bubbling kettle on a hob
to make customers' tea?

the walk's taken hours; Wendy caculates
ground covered, territory conquered,
spottable spots spotted

Feet up, we watch Miranda, again, with Bruce Forsyth
all teeth and white hair, an old vaudevillean who wasn't
to our current knowledge, a molester

also a bio of Ang (gh) ela Merkell
a good egg, solid, not hard-boiled,
Presbyterian-reared, consensus-bent

weathering a long term in office
such as we fickle Brits and colonials
might do well to consider

Moses the cat
sits on the mat, as cats do
keeping us ageless company

6.

The Dying Light

Poll Tax Riots, 1990
In your face, Thatcher

what is the German word for 'ragamuffin'?
I'm watching *Eggheads*, who say *hoodlums*
my brain: a Petri dish of culture

I miss England
now I'm planted firmly back here
what is a knocker-upper's knocker-upper?
you can have too much Fry

nor will I be calling the midwife
then again, I don't read American novels
unless I have to

I liked Siri Hustvedt but she's as good as Swedish

Now Adelaide rolls out the red carpet for the Royal Couple
    you're a little bit of fluff, as one of the nuns said to one of my sisters
        Kate may have heft, but how would you know?

    one will soon be able to visit London's Uniqlo
    a Japanese franchise, but still – when it opens its flagship
    in Melbourne ... a homeopathic dose

        Today, two circuits of the block on foot
        ten on the bike, around and
            around we go, at the bottom of the world

six months in a leaky brain

salvaged facts, wavering convictions
wearing thinner over the course of a day

higher gas bills soon

three kilograms of the drug ice seized

man kills his two little daughters
    that tricky quick brown fox disappears
                with a flick of his russet tail
                        a quavering *Tally Ho!* receding into the

distance

7.

split or stay?

Split, an ordinary afternoon,
     observed from a bollard, a place to stay being
         sought and found at one esplanade agency
           after another
       We can have
           the Mihanovic apartment,
      but I have a bad head by now
        suave Maria lets us in, I
    lie down, the others go out for a meal
  Diocletian's city leaves me cold, though that could be the headache

a certain kind of migraine – the 'white' variety –
           that chills the extremities

douses enthusiasm, certainly
        maybe tomorrow
           (ah, Chrissie, always ready to drop a line)

Yuri and Bianca remain in Hvar,
        already I miss those crazy chimneys

I look out across the courtyard, waiting for the diners-out with takeaway

    I see this block houses a Gynaecologist and a Friseur
      would a *friseur* do massage or hair?

The wanderers return
    with food and the story of the surly waiter

who denies the existence of all the drinks on the menu
    No Negroni – *'whatever that is!'* – and brings
        cappuccino instead of Campari

    in this house of a dozen beds
    we each choose one to lie in

the pillows of sparkling Dalmatia beneath our heads
    the citizens still bent beneath the yoke of Empire

    descendants of Roman legionaries serving Cokes
    adding a spit of poison where they can

8.

A Wrong Bus

A wrong bus
from Angel
carries on down Church Street
into Kilburn

where I made landfall
that first time
by the last Northern Line train
a Tuesday night
green sofa cushions on the floor

soft plastic nozzle on a hose
attached to the bath tap
for showers

a garden flat
with area steps

my friend's baby
in a Mothercare pram in
Petit Bateau matelot shirts
lifted and gifted
by a French *amie*

I peer down side streets
that haven't come up in the world

scan the road ahead for a remembered
glass overpass that led
to high-windowed public baths

disconcerted
as we turn onto my road
that they haven't appeared

9.

creatures of the forest

pebble-dash New Forest bungalow
nylon sheets in the guest room
repelling Australian germs

    met by the housewife
    all nerves and perm

    bookended by
    booming Bogey Colonel Dad
    bristling moustaches and
        menacing bonhomie

    Lynne's parents

    a Somerset Maugham set

or Talking to a Stranger, recently aired back home,
    teen Judi Dench as daughter

    each morning I expect to trip over protruding

        dead toes from behind the sofa.

In the Forest, my album shows

antlered deer and swishing peacocks

what I retain is   bared teeth and cigars
the huge ceramic panther in the front porch

    my legs fizzing with the urge to run

10.

A Rich Full Life

tablescape

drooping roses near death in a jam jar
dull Ian Rankin in a yellow cover lying upside down
Mongolian phrasebook
sample tube of Sensodyne
Cinema ticket: *The Great Beauty*
opener for the Italian Film Festival
password to Smartygrants
for accessing two hundred applications
business card for Phnom Penh silver and gemstone jeweller
a blue and a black biro
invitation to popup arthouse fundraiser at Goodwood School
receipt for Geranium Leaf Aesop cleanser
Yuri's business card at the Apple Store
its bitten silver apple on gloss white
white enamel teapot with redrimmed lid
remote control for Smart TV
another Scottish crimemeister, Stuart McBride
Close to the Bone, his back to me
at the far end of the table
notebook
this pen

11.

Night Train

Stacey and I,   back
        at Arlo and Moe's

yellow mismatched chairs and tables
bountiful light through many-paned windows
        hip coffee, cool clientele, delectable
            mums, monster buggies
                consuming the space

over the road   Crofton Park Library
(I know to check the books-for-sale rack
one pound or less)

already nostalgic for here

    Stacey's new threesome are repatriating
        closing the door behind them
            to this frequent visitor
            I'll need new *raisons de voyager*

                if I'm spared   a chilling
                parting shot of my Nana's

    what verbal tics of mine
        will they quote?

                best not speculate

baby Noah slept all walk long
allowing us the rambling chat
we'd been saving up

what with her work on borough councils
and the ineluctable rights of a new princeling

He sleeps on, wakes
in his pram five minutes from home

just time to work himself
into a lather of tears
easy soothed with milk
and cuddles

We have a fish pie at Wendy's
for a late supper
when I find my way back
on a Haggerston night train

padding out the
familiar walk
around the park

nod to the pub
in the far corner, dim-lit
Duke of Wellington

squat old corner church
studded timber door
shadowy stone porch

just by the dumpster with its 'bin your knives'
sticker

each of the new houses
in Albion Drive

sits over a hole
left by a bomb

too-new false teeth in the venerable row

hers, a genuine faux-Georgian
spared, lived on
to welcome Wendy as the 80s dawned

nudging its bicentennial,
more des-res than ever in its life

the 10.30 night train bore
mostly couth travellers

returning from dinners
parties and gigs

At Haggerston
all the white folks
hive off towards the Mill
Apartments,

newly-completed
still draped in banners

boasting proximity to the canal,
five minutes' walk

so lately the haunt
and maybe still
    of 'footpads'

I trot eastwards
E8: Hackney's zipcode
from the tube station

itself brand-new, wide entrance
broad empty hall, soaring ceilings,
bright lights, new-heroic mosaics
perforated silver metal seats

you can see for miles
in both directions from the new platform

On the fridge back home sits a photo of Stacey
sitting on it, waiting for the train

cradling a potted palm
for their then new house
the one before this one

I turn left at the top of the park
in company with the hoodies
quicken my pace involuntarily
though I tell myself I feel secure
let myself deftly in with my key

follow the scent of cat
down to the kitchen

12.

Perambulation

The wheels
on the pram
go round
and round
pudgy toes visible
from behind and above
a short index finger
extended at intervals
to points of interest
Old Macdonald's chorus
floats back from
beneath the canopy
a jaunty 'Moo!'
the walk enlivened
by passing dogs
diving birds
a white cat stock-still
dead ahead on the path
flowers between fence slats
requiring investigation

The day breaks open
displays its flesh

13.

River Run

I read Jenny's Wellington poems again
    her friends are constant
flourishing by the Derwent
    season to season

by Hobart's Derwent, some of mine
    from half a life ago have blossomed
        unwatered by visits from me, more deeply
    channelled, more tangled

into themselves, nourished by their gardens
    even while they dug them

melding themselves into their houses of sticks
    clay, stone, rearing children

making livings, earning livelihoods
    sending fledglings out into the world

when, one fine day, I come back, they put the kettle on

with tea we wash the dust of long roads
    from our throats
        the sky shines over the southern edge of the world
    clouds scud over our heads

        we acknowledge with better grace now
the onward tug of the river, pulling us with it
    as it runs along by

14.

Allingham at Abney Park

Fed Wendy's cat, walked to Broadway
Market through London Fields

a month from now these will be
once again names to conjure with

jump on a 236
Newington Green
lured by the memory
of *Belle Epoque* patisserie
glowing golden in a corner

always misremembered

as *Raisin D'Etre*

My fellow-travellers clearly
locals despite farflung origins
even on my ninth visit
I'm a day-lily among annuals

When I'm seated at my table
the *escargot* pastry is perfect
the coffee not

c'est la vie

From Wendy's bookshelf
I've taken *Death of a Ghost*
Margery Allingham
best-loved Dame of Crime

died a year younger
than my present age

so many books!
beneath an unflattering
photo, her Green Penguin blurb
'In my family, it would have
seemed strange not to write'

yet I know no other Allingham

my internal satnav (not the *Epoque
vendeuse*'s doubtful directions) tells me

Church Street is nearby
Abney Park cemetery therefore
in walking distance, a favourite for

the unchecked frivolity
of its riot of nameless
creepers and saplings

gobbling tumbled memorials
rampaging madly on

my lately-penned Will specifies
eco-burial, probably in a polite park

better this rampant decay under
thrusting, immodest new growth
the Victorian way

en route to last things, I detour
via penultimate ones

a light-filled ex-factory
scuffed wooden floors
raised platform at the back
sparse, select items dangling at intervals
and in the wide window

a light-as-air linen swingcoat
faintest oyster blue-grey
made for a small man my size
not too many pounds asked,

enthuse with the attendant
who seems as charmed as I
by the garment, as perhaps she is
leave empty-handed

In the cemetery I peer through a screen of oak leaves
squint at the flat Yuri had, with Teresa the mad landlady
a few years back, overlooking this tangle of rubble
deepest green shade

the passage of years
sickeningly vertiginous
when it's your childrens' years

you're reckoning, let alone
amongst tombstones

outside *Epoque* earlier,
two girl cyclists hugged goodbye

stalwart in Birkenstocks,
tortoise-shelled by Freitag backpacks
full of calm and poise
grounded as I wasn't

I thought of my reading at their age
how I longed for each new
Drabble, bound to be bursting
with important

tips for living my modern life

all forgotten

Margaret is coming
to Writers Week, I'm reading
her new books, elderly heroes
all passion spent

while Margery's spectral tale from 1934,
in my backpack, is a painter's story
'Lafcardio, RA'
Royal Academician

my ghosts today are clamorous
not unfriendly

15.

Island Time

banded bumble bees already at work
by 6 am in the rosemary

slaters still hovercrafting over the bathroom floor
not realising the sun's up

not a shrug of wind in the garden
the surface of the sea
taut-stretched grey marle

yesterday, the pair of sea eagles
flew above the car, keeping pace
for a bit as I drove

an escort of black-and-whites
on your way, ma'am
nothing to see here

16.

Song for Joni

A character on a page that falls open in my book says
        'Come here, you fruitcake!'

addressing
        'the kind of boy who could grow into a malcontent
            or a leader of men'

  I go outside to weed around the orange tree,
      fingers unerringly dislodging
         hidden dog turds,
      amazed at the potency of my free-floating rage
         Mad as hell.

  The dog sits three feet away, wishing the sun would go down
      so it would be dinner time
         she tries out a half-hearted whine or two

Joni Mitchell's song from 'Blue' floats out from inside:

California, comin' home ...

such a pretty voice, but isn't she Canadian?

    the angles of her face in that deep-indigo album-cover shot
    Navajo planes and hollows, scooped and sculpted
        the chords take me back to dangerous times
        Turn this crazy bird around
           shouldn'a got on this flight tonight

here comes my flown-away brother:

wish I had a river I could skate away on ...
           hope you've got your heat turned on

the river pulls me down, everything pools and puddles

Tasmanian backroads, houses on hillcrests, cold water in creeks,

wind-blasted pines, cold striking through Kombi-van walls at four in the
afternoon

little boys in hand-knits and corduroys and gumboots, arms stretched

to catch the sun, a ball,

the falling air

I go inside and scrub the sink with Gumption

the quaver in Joni's voice goes through you like a knife through butter

I focus on the bee made of yellow wooden discs

on the record cabinet

wiggling her twig antennae

sniffing through her red-bulb nose

shouldn'a got on this flight tonight

17.

Suburban Moments

1

election posters go up
around the neighbourhood
Family First has two
jolly men, side by side
Now that's nice

the Green candidates share
a grey pallor: low-res photos
underscoring their worthiness

Terina Monteagle standing
for the Liberals in our electorate
sounds like a sports car or
a mountain climber

Annabel Digance is a
good name for a Labor politician
who'd call a spade
a spade, and know how to use it

2

Linh Chi beauty salon has opened
in the shopping mall that grew up
around our favourite supermarket

at Pasadena, whose Californian
aspirations I love

the beauticians squat in rows
at our feet, chatting to one another
in Vietnamese as they wash, buff
and polish our toes

'Choose a colour', they call
to one woman after another
as we straggle in,
footsore

3
From where I sit on the verandah
I can hear but not see
the postman arrive on his scooter
the squeak and clatter of the mailbox lid
being lifted and dropped

if the sun wasn't shining so warmly
on my ankles, I'd check the post

instead try to gauge
the length of the shoots on the new
Geraldton Wax by the verandah post
gaining ground where its predecessor failed
too gnarly and bent to walk under
the fresh needles a searing citron
the picture of health

4
This morning I put on face cream
left hand to right cheek
right hand to left
could be the charm

trees shake out their hair
in a gentle breeze
exhale, a sigh of relief
stretch out metatarsals
in cool, damp soil
after the wettest February days
in fifty years, following on
the hottest ditto

carefully selected
they're local to the area

you'd think we might thrive
in the soil that grew us
show adaptations
to its mineral content

my lungs are still Irish
five generations on
prefer damp bog air
to Adelaide dry

5.
I pull into my driveway
catch my neighbour neatly, unhurriedly emptying

a carton of plane leaves around the Golden Rain tree
      in the middle of our stretch of verge

verge verger *vergogna*

vergogna: shame, what I feel a rush of
for why? The huge plane on our joint boundary
eighty or ninety years old, sheds papery, indestructible leaves
      they rain on us and neighbours alike

I sweep up and bin Peggy's deposit

plotting how, under cover of darkness
I might encourage our dog to shit on her strip of gravel
      wondering which of us will die first

6.
Admiring our string of pinprick fairy lights
draped in swags around the living room
Ashley, our tenant-gardener's cousin, describes
the 100-watt ones his cousin got from Bunnings where he works
for a friend to use at a party: when turned on, they were so bright
'it was like the Ark of the Covenant being opened'

Lo, now there is a mystery attached to Ashley
did he have a religious upbringing, or does he, like me
retain a vivid memory of that scene in 'Raiders of the Lost Ark'?

I could ask him, but in trying to frame the question
the moment has passed

18.

Mangle-Worzel

Back at Cranfield Street by 5
Motorway horridness receding into fumey oblivion
just in time for *Pointless* – words ending in 'air'
'debonair'? – others, phoned at random, knew that one

Two pounds fifty left on my Oyster card once I've dashed through the barrier
and across the delicately high-slung white and black painted
timber-floored pedestrian bridge over the Brockley line

all along the route is densely wooded with lanky elder saplings
dock and nettles, layers of green petticoats below the asphalt belt

Wendy's raspberries are flourishing in her damp back garden
I only notice the hundreds of orb spiders strung on webs between the bushes
when I come eye to eye with one as I bend to gather fruit

Brockley Market turns two on Saturday: I'll be there.

travel, the scavenger's best excuse: every find a clue
to the answer you've been seeking
I've acquired a copy of *Worzel Gummidge*
  'Do tell us how you came alive?'
  '... so far as I can mind, it all started with a itching in the head,
  when the turnip began to sprout.'

Three Oxford Children's Modern Classic authors
ring bells, from the list on Worzel's fly-leaf

Rosemary Sutcliff, Philippa Pearce, Astrid Lindgren

I know the TV Gummidge, not the book
or its author, Barbara Euphan Todd
who 'started writing when she was eight', the little swot

the written story's charm
a mirthless tale of mud, muddle and mayhem
eludes me

　　　Why do I love England? And yet I do.

19.

half-cocked

first time away
first port, Athens
arrivals hall, armed
welcoming committee

guns slung
casually across
khaki chests

welcomed to the city
by leering labourers
leaning sideways out
of scaffolding

everything either
half-built or
half-collapsing

a man half-hidden
in park bushes
exposing half
of himself

another making a grab
on the scenic track
up the back of
the Acropolis

I flail him away with
 a picket plucked
from a fallen fence

Claire, who runs
my British pension
offers shuttered
windows

and deep baths
where I soothe
distended breasts

round rebukes
from their intended
beneficiary, half
a world away

my lewd gestures
make sense to
the chemist, who

dispenses
remedies, their
demotic language

blessedly readable
by my internal
codebreaker

Of Delphi
I recall a long room
of shards under glass

and the bronze boy
I'd loved
from afar

his green stare
disdaining
half-measures

20.

Take a chance on us

The spacecraft Rosetta detaches a module
flings it hopefully at an approaching comet
aiming for the 'clinging-on spot'

the samples it might collect
will test the theory that life on earth
arrived via meteorite

in the beginning was the word
and the word was 'asteroid'
and eventually 'world'

that lovely portmanteau
carbon atoms, volcanic gases, bangs and fizzes
in the beginning was the beginning

Here in the church-hall cafe
adjoining the Anglican ladies' jumble
a timewarp Barbara Pym scene, hangs a poster

of Noah's Ark: jolly, up-and-doing Mrs Noah
up to her stout armpits in dung, doubtless,
usual crew of wildlife peering through portholes

the dove hovering above in a blue sky
all floating over the drowned, sinful world
Jehovah wiping the slate clean

exepting Noah, a boozy old
lech, best sire God could find
for a new breed

The module has hit the target, amazingly
clinging on for dear life like the Ark on Mount Ararat
scooping data-rich dirt to be decoded

into a new word for the new millennium
the word is Chance
and a fine thing it is

21.

Super Maria Brothers

the priests and the witchdoctors both
will bless your new vehicle; the Virgin
will keep you in mind if you fashion a model
of what you want, attach it to the front of the car

> a second storey on your house
> a house pure and simple
> a swinging baby doll
> attached to your grille

'The Virgin won't give them anything'
shrugs Father Abraham: it'll be hard work
gets the second storey or the first
good luck or bad that delivers or
    withholds babies

> The medicine men pooh-pooh the minimal
> offices of the Friars – they themselves offer
> in addition to the basic plan, prayers to the earth gods
> thrilling rituals and holy smoke

the camera pans round a wall of wax engravings
for the attention of the Virgin of Copacabana

here, our gurus advise visualising
what we desire:

      a private welter of wants

            I like the Bolivian way
          heart on your sleeve, swinging dice
         buffeting the rearvision mirror
     a decade of the rosary, a burnt offering
          hey! down here! we'll take anything!
         a shout-out to whoever's online

22.

Carlo Victor Bornholdt

on unearthing his old birth notice

With a name like that
he's bound to become a Professor of Something

the morphology of glacial rocks
the chemistry of underwater volcanic gases
moral philosophy

on the way there he will solve stacks of Sudoku puzzles
crates of cryptic crosswords

but still be the kind of boy who gets the jokes
in *Wayne's World*

his girlfriend's name will be Ottoline
                              or Ada
            he will retain his taste for little pasta shapes

think fondly and often of his brother, Felix
who plays jazz piano in that famous New York bar
                        where Woody Allen plays blues

never forget his mother, or the home-baked bread
            he learned to make himself

the number of times each day the coffeepot was set

to boil on the white-enamelled stovetop

23.

Magic Possum

first, we began to notice hollow globes
flesh emptied through neat holes
like eggs sucked by stoats
(as I imagine)

mid-summer, the late-fruiting tree is bare
trunk deep in brown, hard grenades

it's a new trick, in our time here
for a species we underestimated

more rats than usual, too, this winter and spring,   the
nonchalant boulevardier on the outermost pergola spar
joined by a rush of fellow-commuters

afternoon sun catches in their pink gnocchi ears
    sitting pretty: grape, sour cherry, plum
        lines on supermarket shelves

    birds snaffle green almonds at birth
    loquats likewise

        we feed the beasts of the field
        the birds of the air, who toil not
            neither do they spin,

                saving
                    our Heavenly Father the bother

the rats speed around the rails
sure as carriages round a train track
smarter by the season
sleeker by the day

their only competition the possums
in the race to inherit the earth

24.

Ragtime

Thirteen years over the water
now Gabe, Stace and Noah
move in across the road

catching the same bus into town
shopping at the same supermarket
Gabe grew up with

I hear a bus go by : is it 'on the up'
or 'on the down' ? transport-worker-speak
familiar since buses began tannoying

calls to and from the depot. Noah hears
trains from a suburb away
remarks on them all. Newly-sensitised, we

note every faint toot in some vague mental log
Today, having a tiny fever, I wear a thick jumper
and thongs, waiting for Stacey to collect

my ragbag, proudly full of
torn-up sheets, old nappies and towels,
undies and singlets, all cotton

when the call comes, I'm Girl-Guide prepared

hanging from the pergola, autumn leaves are
a dazzling fire curtain against the afternoon sun

shading into russet brown, slated for pruning
a clear outlook   -   clairvoyance

The parrots who raided the pecan tree have 'flown away'

advises Noah, illustrating with outflung arms
we are scavenging their leavings, unshucked nuts
a call to future-proofing

life in this house sparking up again, thinking ahead
rather than simply 'doing the needful' (an Indian-anglicism
current back in London, Gabe says)

Until someone comes knocking, stacked provisions
are a reproach: right this second,
there's a tap at the door.

25.

Mumbai Shuffle

In a famous Mumbai slum, Kevin McCloud
gravely ponders a million souls in a square mile
producing millions' worth of goods
apparently from nothing

women in doorways lean in towards each other
not everyone smiles at Kevin, or, beyond him, at us
in our odourless dwellings, with no more rats than we can handle
toilets to shit in rather than the open drains their kids dangle over

on a hot night in Adelaide
one dead rat is making its olfactory mark nearby
a lone cockroach crosses the floor
it's the season when the eye catches sideways scuttles

the lizard brain hisses 'arachnid'
before the front elaborates: 'huntsman'

I may be alone in all this space
but absent family clusters round

we slept five to a room when small
sharp edges ground down by proximity, rubbing along

in the slum, the streets are safe at night
at parties, ten or more pairs of hands touch your food
before your plate reaches you

the schoolgirls leaving these warrens each new day
are crisp as banknotes
clean as whistles
which do not follow their shining progress

26.

Spring Carnival

bedroom curtains drawn against sun on
    the first day of spring

      someone's tripped a switch
almond blossoms submerge beneath foliage
      wattle froth, yellow-silver, bubbles way above the fence

woody plants struck on the local columnist's advice
    cling on like billy-oh

      six clay pots of healthy herbs in a huddle on the verandah

      lively portents for matriarch Moira's 90th
          at the racecourse, perfect choice for a stayer
          and lifelong punter

in wedding photos beamed up on the reception room wall
        tall, lean, composed, clever eyes
    older-than-usual newlywed
      upon Jack's safe delivery from Palestine and Pacific
under the starter's gun for the Catholic wives' handicap
on her mark to race God's steeplechase
here are all her sons and daughters, and theirs, and theirs
        At ninety, she may reconsider
          rising at five
          in favour of six

one-time telephonist at GPO Central Exchange
    still plugs in to endless bulletins
hold please, connecting you now

electricity snakes down her fingers, old RKO-style
      transmitting worldwide
         volts of sympathy, sense, silliness, straight-talk
      she danced in the Post Office Follies
         Tap on, Moira Jane
               tap on

27.

Dog's Breakfast

under the orange tree
            tartan rug, pillow, pencil, strewn bones: new dog's work
      autumn light, pinkish gold, afternoon slipping into evening
          on the rug, a book within a book, hardback slipped between
                                   journal pages

Retrieving them, I find new dog has chewed apart the notepad covers
      neatly excised a third of a page from the hidden text
                now digesting data on Joseph Stalin's
obsession with blondes, blondeness, fair hair and blue eyes

  Pola herself is black and beautiful (know your Old Testament, Joe?)

    Zorro mask, black coat, white muzzle and legs
         new dog regards me with her ice-blue stare
          – all grist to my mill, lady

28.

corked

Cork Youth Hostel
late arriving
bedtime bath
Victorian pipes
cop an earful next morning
reply in kind
surprising myself
'rudest man I've ever met'
vows to ring ahead
warn his hostel-cronies
to bar their doors
he's from Manchester
a fact I unconcsciously store
mistrust Mancunians ever after

29.

Hereabouts Haiku

yoga in Scout Hall, Harmony Day art
red maple-leaf, CNANDA

walking-frame alongside highchair
outside op-shop: a concrete poem

30.

These Boots

feeling cosmopolitan in suede desert boots

catch the nine am bus, beating the rush
alight for coffee at Illy, taking the vacant bishop's-throne chair

should think about writers to feature in my rescued program
　　　　instead I contemplate these teddy-boy shoes
　　　　　　　from a kids' store in a toffy mall

kick back in my Monski teeshirt – six pounds in Carnaby Street
　　　　the very day that Danish franchise opened, my last that London
　　　　　　　　　　　　　　　　trip
　　　　funky but cheap, funky but cheap, yeah

Here I am on the hip corner of North Terrace, our cultural boulevard
　　　grey cells on *pause*, music video on the big screen over there
　　　　evergreen Queen, get it on, Freddy

Melbourne, I see, is instating a Jewish Writers Festival
　　　　how about an ex-Catholic one
　　　　　　　　　　hold me back

there'd be crucifixion jokes and Tom Lehrer songs
we'd hold the panel chats in converted churches

recite Life of Brian monologues

trade stories: alcoholic fathers, martyred mothers

light bonfires in the grounds of the abandoned Passionist seminary
burn effigies of popes and cardinals

read Gerard Manley Hopkins to each other in our cups

sing, in the early hours, those favourite hyms we still use to put
ourselves to sleep

31.

Endless Summer

to the beach to swim in a murky sea, storm-stirred
seaweed churned to feathery sludge
softly agreeable underfoot, as far as the sandbank

home to team up with the boys to finally pull down the front verandah ceiling
dating back before our time: white, soft panels that will sit in the yard
till they mulch enough with rain to squash small

decades of detritus descend as we rip them from their moorings
dessicated droppings, pollen bobbles from the plane tree in dusty cascades
revealing for the first time in eighty years the dark cool of terracotta depths

the spine of the roof dimly visible way up high

an unseen hand hacking at the ivy from outside the garden wall
must be Steve, who comes through the gate now, arms full of
sticky marbled fronds to cut up for green waste

more storms tonight, humid heat, dense cloud
sit on the now cloistered porch sofa, watch the noisy mynahs boss and bully
wattlebirds I never manage to like, peewees, blackbirds; wishing for wrens and
robins

our Bruny yardbirds, redbreast puffballs on the wooden fence,
superb blue fairies, thuggish to females
drab fluff-bundles destined for drubbing

down on the shoreline those juiced-up dotterils, cartoon fast-walkers
battery-powered comedians I always accompany, in my head, with Bugs Bunny
tinky-tonk

still, I like our finches, electric-yellow sideburns flashing in the acacia

tempted, now, to hang some token at the new entryway
an octagonal mirror to deflect evil, prayer-flag bunting, image of the Virgin
bird feathers and shells laced into a mobile

only asking for trouble, right?

the house might be mine, but the city's overdue for a quake like the '54
shakedown. Best just let the new dust settle,
sit and think or just sit, Ma

     shotgun broken across the knees

Around Here
Cath Kenneally

Cath Kenneally's poetry is unique: confident, discursive, witty writing driven by intuition and association and a doubting, quick intelligence. With a focus ever-shifting between local, global, present and past, familial and political, Cath draws you into her world with a compelling combination of emotional intensity and clearsightedness.

Winner of the 2002 John Bray National Poetry Prize

For more information visit www.wakefieldpress.com.au

Jetty Road
Cath Kenneally

Jetty Road is an amusing and insightful novel about women of a certain age, kids and oldies – about life actually, and how we never really grow into it. The story explores the intertwined lives of two sisters, Evie and Paula Haggerty. Damaged by their early life experiences – Evie's past drug habit and the collapse of Paula's long-term relationship – the sisters depend on one another to stand strong against the challenges of mid life, and together face difficult decisions that must be made.

For more information visit www.wakefieldpress.com.au

Room Temperature
Cath Kenneally

She and six classmates have announced they'll be joining the nuns when they leave school at the end of the year. The apparent finality of this collective repudiation of the world, in a weird sort of way, is cool.

First-born, eldest daughter, Little Mother to her siblings, Irish-Australian, brainy schoolgirl at the time the Beaumont children vanish … will the real Carmel please stand up? When it comes time to venture into love and other alternatives, mutinous forces undermine her confidence, and malevolence turns to violence. Now she's starring in her own horror-home-movie.

Room Temperature, a mosaic of subtle allusion and canny observation, is a novel about memory, time, and the struggle to break away from family pathology.

For more information visit www.wakefieldpress.com.au

Thirty Days' Notice
Cath Kenneally

This collection forms a day-book of poems, set in various locations, especially Adelaide, Melbourne, Sydney, Wellington, London and Bruny Island (Tasmania), all significant for Cath Kenneally. Reflective, wry and occasionally rude, the poems in *Thirty Days' Notice* have their origins in the everyday, dropping in on backyards and beaches, train stations and airports, cafes and kitchens, provoked by photographs, books and letters, relationships and solitude, an undead Catholic childhood and the pangs and pleasures of motherhood as they ponder what a life of days might add up to.

For more information visit www.wakefieldpress.com.au

Wakefield Press is an independent publishing and
distribution company based in Adelaide, South Australia.
We love good stories and publish beautiful books.
To see our full range of books, please visit our website at
www.wakefieldpress.com.au
where all titles are available for purchase.
To keep up with our latest releases, news and events,
subscribe to our monthly newsletter.

Find us!

Facebook: www.facebook.com/wakefield.press
Twitter: www.twitter.com/wakefieldpress
Instagram: www.instagram.com/wakefieldpress